UNWRITTEN ROUTES

BY: HAPPINESS AHIPATELA

Copyright © 2025 by HAPPINESS AHIPATELA

All rights reserved. No part of this book may be used or reproduced in any form whatsoever without written permission except in the case of brief quotations in critical articles or reviews.

Printed in the United States of America and or Canada

For more information or to book an event, contact :
Info@cojbookz.com

Cover design by HAPPINESS AHIPATELA

ISBN - Paperback: 978-1-998120-76-5

Acknowledgments

I want to sincerely thank Kamelah Blair from COJBOOKZ and The My Black Is Whole Program for their guidance, encouragement, and belief in my journey as a writer. Your leadership and dedication have left a lasting impact on me, not only through your individual support but also through the powerful work you both do within the mentorship organization.

To the entire team behind the mentorship program — thank you for creating a space where young voices are nurtured, challenged, and uplifted. This opportunity to write and share my story has been deeply meaningful, and it would not have been possible without the foundation you've built.

Your commitment to cultivating creativity, confidence, and purpose in emerging writers is something I will always carry with me. I'm grateful for the chance to be part of this experience and the door you opened that allowed this book to be written.

CHAPTER 1
Under The Spotlight

Grade 11, the city's buzz seeped even through closed windows. My parents, strict traditional African immigrants, emphasized school and degrees over cleats and touchdowns. The home we shared with four siblings was too small for dreams of stardom. My father's expectations landed like heavy tackles, my mother's quiet support weighed just as much. I juggled functions equations with sprint drills, chemistry formulas with playbooks, hungry for both academic approval and the roar of the crowd. Their satisfaction felt conditional, earned on report cards or Friday night lights. Dinner was where it all clashed. The rice was always hot, the stew always spicy, and the questions always pointed.

"Did you study today?"

"How many assignments are left?"

Never "How was practice?" Never "How many yards did you rush for?" My little brother would mimic my footwork in the hallway when Dad wasn't watching. My older sister, already off at university, used to sneak me study tips between my game highlights. But my dad? He'd see my helmet on the kitchen counter and sigh like it was holding me back from med school.

"This football," he said one night, tapping his spoon on the table, "it will not feed you. Focus on what matters." I wanted to tell him it did feed me, maybe not my stomach, but my spirit. On the field, I felt seen. I felt real. Sometimes after dinner, when everyone else was watching African shows or on their phones, I'd sneak out back with a ball and a speaker. I'd run cuts in the dark, dodging imaginary defenders under the yellow porch light. Not for recruiters. Not even for my team. Just for me. Flashbacks came easily, the crowd's roar under stadium lights.

The coach was yelling my name after a first down. My teammates are lifting me after a winning play. That feeling like all the doubts, all the pressure, all the silence didn't matter. But then the light would cut off, and I'd hear my mom at the back door, "Come inside. It's late." I'd nod, wipe sweat off my face, and head back in, returning to the world where dreams had curfews. Even in class, I felt like I lived in two worlds. One where I had to prove I was more than an athlete, and one where I had to prove I was good enough to be one. When teachers smiled extra wide at my 80s like it was surprising, I smiled back even wider, like it didn't sting. When my boys joked about scouts and scholarships, I laughed with them, even though my knee hadn't been right since Week 3. But every time I stepped on that field, something clicked. I wasn't chasing escape. I was chasing balance. Some kind of peace between who I wanted to be and who I was told to become.

CHAPTER 2
The First Hit

September's chill brought more than crisp air. A wrong step, a helmet too low, and a tackle that didn't even make sense. My knee buckled before I could even register the hit. The pain wasn't just physical; it was everything crashing at once.

The scholarship.

The dream.

The plan.

Gone? I didn't know yet. But it felt like it.

They helped me off the field, but I didn't need help walking; I needed help breathing. I needed help processing how something I'd worked for my whole life could twist and tear in one second. The whispers started almost immediately.

"He's done."

"Tough break."

"Might lose his spot."

Some of them weren't even quiet about it. I could feel it in the way they looked at me, sympathy from some, hunger from others.

I sat on the sidelines with my leg wrapped in ice and pride wrapped in silence. Everyone was still moving, still practicing, still talking plays. I was stuck in my head.

Isolation wrapped around me tighter than the bandages and compression sleeves. Physio was slow, robotic. A cold room with colder equipment. The trainer tried to make small talk, asked about school, the team, and how I was "feeling."

I gave him what I could:

"Fine."

"It's alright."

"Just trying to get back."

But inside, it wasn't alright.

Every stretch felt like a reminder of what I couldn't do yet. Every beep of a machine felt like a countdown I was losing. Every moment I wasn't on the field, I wondered if people had already moved on. The worst part- I didn't even know who I was without the game. Football wasn't just something I played. It was where I felt enough. Where things made sense. Out here, in the in-between, I didn't know what made me matter.

Even my homies didn't know what to say.

A dap up here. A "you'll bounce back" there,But the conversations didn't feel the same. I stopped going to lunch with them. Stopped cracking jokes in the locker room. I wasn't angry at them. I just didn't know how to be around them when I didn't feel like myself.

At home, no one really brought it up. My dad mentioned it once, telling me this was "a sign from God" to focus on school. My mom just brought more food to my room. No words. Just silence and stew. And still, every night, I dreamed of the game. Of jukes and dives and touchdowns and cheers. Every morning, I woke up to pain and doubt. The first hit wasn't the tackle. It was what came after the silence, the questions, the fear that maybe I'd already peaked.

CHAPTER 3
Conversations With My Homies

It wasn't therapy, but late-night convos at the park or on the curb after ball felt close enough. That's where we unpacked stuff quietly, between jokes and food, over the hum of streetlights and the clank of a basketball rim in the distance.

Branden would always start it off with something dumb.

"If you could only eat one cereal forever, what's it gonna be?" Somehow, ten minutes later, we'd be knee-deep in real talk. Stuff we didn't bring up in class. Things we didn't even fully understand. Things we brushed off during the day. Teachers still asking me, "What's your name again?" like I ain't been in their class since September. That "Where are you from?" question is not just where do you live, but like my skin needed a visa to exist.

Josh, always yapping, had a way of breaking it down without making it heavy. "It's not always loud, bro. Sometimes racism's whispering in your ear, pretending it's just being curious." Branden would nod like he already knew that, but you could see it hit. Caleb, quiet mostly, just listened. You could tell he took it all in.

Happiness, that's my name, always with some unexpected wisdom. "They want us to either be angry or invisible. And if you're neither, they don't know what to do with you."

We'd sit back, pass around chips or some pizza slices, laugh too loud sometimes, and just be. It wasn't about solving anything. It was about naming it.

Naming the weight. The weird moments. The invisible stuff you carry all day. Scars came up. Not just bruises from the game, but other stuff. The kind you don't show off.

Like how it felt being the only Black kid in a class.

Or when your name gets turned into a punchline during attendance and everyone laughs, including you, because it's easier than explaining why it hurts. We didn't always have the right words,but there was comfort in the mess. Comfort in knowing someone else noticed. That you weren't the only one trying to make sense of being seen and overlooked at the same time. We didn't solve everything. We reminded each other we weren't crazy and sometimes, that was enough.

Enough to make it through the week.

Enough to lace up for the next practice.

Enough to face the next comment with your head up.

CHAPTER 4
Fractured Trust

The locker room felt colder. Not temperature-wise, energy-wise. The jokes didn't land the same. The music didn't hit. Something was off. I noticed it during scrimmages. My knee was still taped, but I was cleared to play light reps. The first few snaps were smooth, short routes, handoffs, nothing special. Then came the play. I ran the route clean. Open down the middle. The QB looked me off. Twice. The ball went the other way. A forced throw into double coverage. Picked off.

SK smiled.

Not a "dang, that sucks" smile.

A "that's what you get" smile.

That's when it clicked.

This wasn't just about football anymore.

Back in the locker room, no one said much. Just helmet clinks and towel snaps. The silence after the loss hurt, but the silence after betrayal? That cut deep. I'd been grinding to get back in shape. Showing up early. Staying late. Taking reps I didn't have to. I thought the team saw that. I thought they were rooting for me. But maybe not all of them were.

Coach didn't say anything. Didn't call out the missed read. Didn't ask why I got iced out. Just moved on like it was nothing. Like I was nothing.

Leadership meetings kept happening, without me. I wasn't even told they were going on. So what was I really recovering from — the injury or their trust?

Group chats got dry. People who used to dap me up in the halls started acting brand new.

"Yo, you good?"

"Yeah."

Lies are exchanged like handshakes. I kept thinking: Was I ever really one of them? Or just useful when I was winning games? It made me rethink everything. All the early mornings. All the extra film sessions.

All the "bro" and "fam" talk.

Was it real?

Or just locker room noise? Even at home, I started snapping more. Little things got to me.

Mom was asking if I wanted more food.

Dad is telling me to "stay focused."

My little brother was asking why I wasn't starting anymore.

I didn't have answers. Just questions with no place to land. I sat alone in the change room one night, way after practice. Just staring at the dented locker door in front of me. I wanted to punch it, but I knew it wouldn't change anything.

UNWRITTEN ROUTES

Trust isn't something you notice when it's strong.

You only feel it when it breaks.

And that week, it broke all around me.

CHAPTER 5
Healing Ground

Physio was a battlefield. Not with helmets or pads, with patience. Every session started the same way. Warm compress. The quiet hum of machines in the background. But it wasn't just about fixing my knee. It was about holding myself together when everything else felt like it was falling apart.

The stretches hurt. The exercises made me sweat in places that had nothing to do with effort, more like frustration. Progress felt slow. Days blurred together. Tension lived in my body, not just from injury, but from everything I carried with me: doubt, pressure, silence. My physiotherapist was calm, sharp, and no-nonsense. But she saw through my fake laughs and short answers. One day, after a tough rep, she just looked at me and said:

"You're not weak. You're healing. There's a difference." I nodded like I got it. But it didn't hit until later, on the bus ride home, earbuds in, world turned down. I wrote that line in my notes, right next to: "What if I never get back to where I was?" The next session, she asked how I was doing, not just my knee, but me. I hesitated. She waited. "Feels like... people only see me when I'm winning," I said finally.

She nodded. "Then it's time you start seeing you even when you're not."

We talked between reps sometimes. About pressure. About being Black in spaces where you had to prove your worth twice to be seen half as much. She didn't have all the answers. But she listened like it mattered. That was new. She introduced me to breathing exercises. Meditation. At first, it felt weird, just sitting by myself. But slowly, I started using it. Before class. After arguments at home. In the locker room, staring at my cleats before warmup. I started writing more. Not just about football, but about everything.

The frustration. The small wins. The little reminders that I was more than stats, more than expectations, more than the noise.

Some days, I still struggled. My body remembered every twist wrong, every near-tear. But I also started recognizing the good, that first clean sprint on the treadmill. The day I finally jumped without flinching. The way the sun felt coming through the clinic window while I iced my leg and thought, I'm getting closer.

Closer to healed.

Closer to the whole.

I still had a long way to go. But for the first time in a while, I wasn't scared of the climb.

CHAPTER 6
Reclaiming The Field

The return to practice felt crazy. I showed up quietly, gear in hand, helmet feeling heavier than usual. First jog back, I felt every eye on me, some curious, some waiting to see if I'd fold. My knee held. Barely. But I kept moving.

The first run was a little off. Coach didn't say much, just nodded. That meant more than a whole speech. Every sprint, every drill, felt like shaking off rust, not just from my body, but from my confidence. My teammates didn't know whether to dap me up or keep their distance. Some did both. But slowly, things shifted. On water breaks, someone cracked a joke about my limp. I laughed with them. Then cooked them in a drill. Light work. Back in the locker room, I didn't just sit and stay quiet. When someone said my name wrong, I corrected them. When a teammate said, "You talk white," I didn't brush it off this time.

"Nah, I just talk. You hear it how you want."

They didn't say it again. Even small stuff, the way coaches overlooked me for a rep, or the way certain dudes side-eyed my reps like I wasn't still that guy, I felt it all. But I didn't let it swallow me. I answered it by showing up by showing out. Game day hits differently. Crowd noise, bright lights, the smell of fresh-cut turf, all of it wrapped around me like home. My name on the speaker. My cleats are digging into the ground. First snap, nerves buzzing. Second play, first touch.

I didn't try to do too much. Just made my reads, took the yards the defence gave, felt the rhythm return to my feet. One cut, then another. Whispers turned to cheers. Doubt turned to daps. After the game, someone slapped my back and said, "You're really back, huh?" I just smiled. Not all the way. Just enough.

Because I wasn't fully back yet. But I was close. And I knew who I was now, not because of the game, but because of everything I fought through to get back to it.

CHAPTER 7
Off-Field Plays

Summer found me where I least expected, not on the turf, not under stadium lights, but inside a gym at the community centre. No cleats. No helmet. Just a whistle around my neck and a group of kids who looked at me like I had all the answers.

At first, I thought it'd be simple. Show up, run some drills, make sure no one gets hurt, and clock out. But it turned into something way deeper.

These kids, wide-eyed and loud, brought energy I hadn't felt since before the injury. Some wore slides too big, jerseys with no names on the back, but they ran every cone drill like scouts were watching. I saw myself in them, that hunger, that spark, just waiting for someone to believe in them.

One kid, Zion, couldn't get a drill right all week. Kept

dropping passes, kept looking over his shoulder like he expected someone to laugh. After one session, he stayed behind, bouncing the ball against the wall.

"You think I'm trash?" he asked. That hit different. I saw myself in that question. That same voice I'd wrestled with when I was injured, when I sat on the bench, or when teachers looked surprised I aced the test.

"Nah," I told him. "I think you're still warming up."

His face shifted. Not a full smile, just enough to let me know he heard me. Next session, he caught every pass. Not clean, not perfect, but with confidence. And that mattered more.

Those small moments added up. Every time I corrected their footwork or showed them how to plant and cut without tearing up their knees, I was giving them more than technique. I was giving them pieces of the playbook life had written for me, one where failure didn't mean finish, and setbacks didn't cancel dreams. Off the field, they asked questions, too.

"Do you think I could go pro?"

"Do people still get racist to you?"

"What if my parents don't care about sports?"

I didn't have perfect answers. Just real ones. Told them sometimes it ain't about going pro, it's about what the game teaches you. Discipline. Guts. Teamwork. How to show up even when no one's cheering.

Told them yeah, racism still shows up, in comments, in assumptions, in silence. But we don't shrink. We stand taller.

Told them even if your parents don't get it now, keep working. Let your dedication speak louder than arguments.

That summer became a mirror. Every lesson I gave them came back to me. I started writing more. Stretching better. Speaking with intention. I stopped waiting for other people's validation, teammates, coaches, even my dad, and started owning my story. Not just the athlete version, but the full version. The mentor. The big bro. The one who knew what it meant to break and still rebuild.

Football brought me into that space. But mentorship made me stay. It wasn't just about training the next generation, it was about healing my own.

CHAPTER 8
The Next Play

The stadium lights hit differently when you know nobody expected you to be here. Not your teachers, not the recruiters who barely glanced your way. From the feeling that I had to prove something just to exist. It didn't matter how many yards I rushed or how many touchdowns I scored. Off the field, I was just another Black kid trying to figure out where I fit. And that? That was the hardest game I've ever had to play. But now, I know. I still lace up my cleats. Not for the scouts. Not for my dad. Not even for the scoreboard. I lace them up for me. The early morning breeze hits differently when you're not chasing approval, when you're just chasing the best version of yourself. The turf under my feet feels like home again, not a test.

I don't need a stadium full of noise to feel like I belong anymore. Some mornings it's just me, a ball, and the echo of my own breath, steady, focused, calm. I've been bruised, benched, and overlooked. But I've also been lifted, trusted, and finally seen. That silence after injury? It taught me how to listen to myself. Those convos with the homies? They taught me I wasn't alone.

The tension in my house? It taught me love doesn't always come easy, but it still shows up, sometimes in the form of a hot meal, sometimes in a stern look that says, "I believe in you, even if I don't say it right."

I still get misjudged. Still get the "you speak so well" looks. Still catch people flinching when I walk past them in a hoodie. That part hasn't changed. But I have.

I speak up now.

I correct people.
I take up space.
This isn't the end of my story. It's just the next play. Whether I make it to U Sports, the NCAA, or end up coaching little

kids in a community gym, I know football didn't just give me a dream; it gave me a mirror. It showed me who I am when everything's stripped away. And who I am is enough. Grades still matter. Dreams still matter. But I don't need to trade one for the other anymore. I've found the balance, not perfectly, not always, but enough to keep moving forward without breaking.

People used to look at me and only see potential. Now, I look in the mirror and see progress. So yeah, the lights hit different now.

Not because they shine brighter, but because I finally know who's standing in them.

Post-Game Thoughts This wasn't just about football. It never was. It was about identity. Pressure. Doubt. And what it means to grow up with dreams that feel too big for the space you're given.

Writing this made me realize how much I was carrying, and

how much I wasn't saying out loud. Sometimes, we brush things off just to keep going. But silence can pile up. And if you never unpack it, it starts to weigh more than the pads ever did.

To anyone who's ever felt like they had to prove themselves just to belong, in a classroom, on a field, even in their own home, I see you. I was you. Maybe I still am, some days. But I'm learning that showing up as yourself is already enough. Choosing your own lane, even if it's not the one people expected, is a win on its own.

This story isn't wrapped in a perfect bow. That's real life. But the growth is there. The work is still happening. And I'm proud of that.

If you took anything from this, whether it was a reminder, a new thought, or just a moment where you felt seen, then that means something. That's the kind of win that sticks.

This was my way of reclaiming the narrative.

Yours might look different. But it matters just as much.

Keep playing. Keep growing. Keep being YOU.

– Happiness

www.ingramcontent.com/pod-product-compliance
Lightning Source LLC
Chambersburg PA
CBHW071232160426
43196CB00012B/2488